Almost Said, Almost Stayed

The Words I Couldn't Say, and the Love That Almost Was

Sindoori

BookLeaf Publishing
India | USA | UK

Made with ❤ on the BookLeaf Publishing Platform
www.bookleafpub.in
www.bookleafpub.com

Dedication

This book is dedicated to ***you***, the one who never asked for these words but , unknowingly became the reason I wrote.

~to the someone i could never muster courage to open up to

If u knew all these......would you still leave?

Preface

This collection of poems began as a silence- a silence I could never conquer, no matter how hard I tried .These poems are just pieces of what I could never say when I had the time .It is not a love story, but rather a story of what happens when love is left unsaid. It's about the distance between two people who were never able to speak their truths, whose unspoken words became the spaces they couldn't bridge. It's about the pain of losing something before you ever had the chance to fight for it, and the quiet acceptance that comes after .This is my attempt to turn the things I never had the courage to say into something that might live on

only if you had seen me crying on the floor -you would believe love exists

~every word i couldn't say
became a poem

Acknowledgements

To everyone who has ever loved in silence ,felt a lot yet were never able to express, to the people who were broken in pieces that couldn't be spoken, and still found the strength to move forward—***this book is for you***

a special thank you to the person who unknowingly became my reason for writing .Though you might never read these words, know that they exist because of you.
~to the one I never had the courage to speak to

*my parents who supported me throughout and are the sole reason ,who encouraged me to publish this...**it means a lot!***

*last but definitely not the least my biggest supporter-my best friend who took time to read the drafts and help me, and to all my friends who stood by my side through the darkest of times....**I LOVE YOU ALL***

THE PAST

This is not a poem ,but my diary indeed,
stripped open all my wounds in this.
For those who love me this might be hard to read,
but those who hate, get ready for a treat.

Let's start this story somewhere in the middle,
as my past is an unsolvable riddle,
but I feel it is a part of who I am,
the currents of my ocean and how I swam.

Just a normal girl who thought life was a bliss,
love was all about a warm hug and a kiss.
now that I think back I do realize,
it's that exact me that I dearly miss.

Excited to fly and yet too scared,
entered a place with a lot of weird stares.
"*is there something wrong with me?*", asked myself,
if I am happy or gloomy don't know why nobody cared.

That little girl tried soo hard to fit in,
to not let all those insecurities creep in,
but as much a she hated it.....
the walls became a part of her living.

She tried her best to make everyone smile,
but in turn a lot of her pains she'd hide.
Sooner or later this became the norm,
"*if it makes them happy then what's the harm?*".

Sending love gets you some,
that was what the world told her.
Writing songs and a weird hum,
as paper was the only one who listened there.

She still had that hope deep in her mind,
"*If I give more, they could be mine!*".
But some people are just not meant to be yours,
I wish I knew that when i had the time.

COST OF CALING THEM FRIENDS

Met all those people and made them laugh,
they did too, it was less, but enough.
The craving for love was put to an end,
when I had a person I could call my friend.

Talked for hours till they gained my trust,
but even the prettiest pillars can get some rust,
if not taken care of as you should've.
wilting flowers are the prettiest first.

People made me laugh all my life,
before pushing me into darkest of hives.
That is why I suggest-not to fall for their lies,
or if you do pls pay the price.

Had people I would call my friends
trusted a lot, handed secrets to them,
But one day all of it came crashing down,
and this is where the sweetness ends.

And that is where the darkness starts,
the lies and the tears and the broken past,
the one which i thought would forever last,
in my mind as big as a mast.

"You are ugly and a liar oh! look at you!"
"How bad you are, you have no clue!"
"You should be thankful we even talk to you!"
and the 12 year old thought maybe it was true.....

THE BETRAYAL

"*we would never let out our secrets*" we had a rule,
one fine morning when I went to school,
found all my secrets were turned into a joke,
and maybe for breaking me that was the first tool.

Whispers reached before I could,
close my ears, still could hear.
I wanted to scream "**I AM MISUNDERSTOOD!**"
but it was of no use so still I stood.

Ran to the bathroom as fast as I could,
making sure no one saw my eyes flood.
the moment so piercing it made me feel,
better than betray was the bright red blood.

Amidst the sobs I still managed to hear,
them laughing, their taunts ever so clear.
I tried my best to be strong,
but I just fell there...gasping for air.

Still in their eyes not a bit of care,
a pinch or regret in their eyes was rare.
that's when I saw my vision blur,
and dripped every one of that tear.

"Why did she cry we don't even know"
was what that little girl heard when she was all alone.
And somehow she managed to hide the next tears,
and run home to cry in her room alone.

I was left wondering "*what was my fault?*",
I always did what was right- I thought.
"*maybe i am not worthy of love*"
these are all the questions it brought.........

A CURSE OR A BOON?

Now I understand why I am this way,
why I fear the night during the brightest of days.
Why I do feel, but I never say,
why in between the whites and blacks, I crave grey.

Why trust someone just to get hurt?
why love someone just to be burnt?
I still cant believe how I was in the past,
and what remained was just a cold heart.

I vowed not to love anymore ,
not to go through the pain I felt before.
not to give it my all,
as they'll always want more.

I don't know if it was the hurt or the fear,
I promised not to go back to that horror.
Not to make someone a reflection of me,
so that I can never look in the mirror.

Life went on-lost those people,
life seemed fine but just not right.
It felt as if I was missing a ripple,
the one that looks prettier at night.

But little did I know that it would end soon,
a new chapter of my life and I was over the moon.
a chapter that would leave me questioning,
if life was a curse or was it a boon?

THEM

The day I saw a glimpse of them,
felt I knew all yet none of them.
stood in front, was a familiar stranger,
no past, but yet to make a future.

Staring when they looked back,
to screaming at their set backs,
it was weird to feel so much,
when you didn't know who they were.

A smile to light my world,
and a glimpse to make me swirl.
Oh boy! did they have it all,
but kept me wondering who they are.

Nothing much happened per se,
just caught me red handed-
staring at them!
but not how you think might I say.

Not something which I thought in my wildest dreams,
a look into their eyes and they made it seem,
I was the prettiest thing they laid eyes on,
a high they would forever wish to stay on.

It was as magical as it could be,
the way our feelings superimposed,
oh to be loved without a remorse,
they were everything I could ever hope for.

LOVE

Fell in love for the first time, o boy it felt good!
after years of being called unlovable and rude.
Nobody really looked into my eyes,
if they did, they would see whatever they should.

Its not up to me what I do or I say,
if it was i would never hurt anyone per se.
but the irony of my life true to this day,
for the people who hurt, hurt those who cared..

This time it was different in the best possible way,
one who could effortlessly make my heart sway..
who used to do more than just say,
who loved me as they wanted to and not to just stay.

I loved them! more than anyone to this day,
a feeling so ecstatic I cant even explain,
all my walls broken piece by piece,
like the dust, after the rain.

Life was good, amazing infact !
forgot all those visions of past,
maybe they were the one I was searching so far,
the one I could go to when things were bizarre.

Life with them felt amazing,
the girl who never thought of her future,
started planning everything silently.
They did too...just a bit more openly,
while she smiled seeing their visions align beautifully.

we would make a great pair! she thought,
still processing all those feelings she caught.
the girl who never cared about birthdays or dates,
seemed to have a special date she never forgot...

ECHOES OF PAST

The next meet however was a bit panicking,
the past visions kept trafficking.
don't trust! they say as trust breeds hurt,
all those pretty flowers wilt into dirt.

Tried so hard ,yet not enough,
couldn't get close without feeling rough.
Trauma makes u bloom-like a lotus,
hate the dirt but cant grow without it.

Wanted to say a lot yet kept quiet,
loved a lot but just silent,
kept a smile with thoughts so violent,
it was hard to be a stream they wanted,
when your mind itself was a torrent.

Pushed them away wanting them close...
pricked them with thorns trying to give them the rose...
Trust me I have every bit of remorse...
but I couldn't fight the demons of past as they rose.

Their patience was something I never felt before,
coming back with a smile when I needed them most.
They knew very well my past was a terror,
but still stuck with me as if I'm their only resort.

The guilt of not being who I wished to be,
Of loving them as freely as they loved me.
To make them smile like they did to me,
I would die just to see me doing these....

SILENT LOVE

Loved them more than anyone else,
yet stayed away as my defense.
Defense from what? you may ask,
if you've been hurt it the past, this will make sense.

The helplessness of loving so hard ,
yet expressing so little.
Them thinking-u never loved them,
and just stayed so they don't get sad.

When all you want is to love them,
rather show them how you are.
They've never seen my diaries filled with words,
as ink is better than those body scars..

Hated myself for being not enough,
to not love them when I wanted that much,
amidst of trying to be in the toughest of times..
maybe I was never there when the sun shined.

Don't get me wrong I loved them like sun to the moon!
so close and yet so far ,love so different yet at par.
Cheering from the background hoping they'll get it soon,
making them so special, more than any other star.

Couldn't watch them in gloom without tearing my eyes,
would burn like the sun just to light up their eyes,
all these feeling were such a surprise,
never knew I was destined for all of these highs.

I knew they were hurt and it hurt me bad....
to see them silent when I didn't want them to be sad,
I was the one supposed to make them smile!
but maybe I couldn't with whatever I had....

THE CHANGE

What could i do? i was trying me best,
to not hurt that heart in which I liked to rest.
To be the peace that they need the most,
and not the one who made them feel the worst.

I don't know if I hurt them or not,,
the curse is-*maybe I will never find out,*
to not love openly was never a choice...
wish I could tell u before things went south...

Loved them too much to give up so easily,
hence fought my battles slowly but surely.
I could feel myself improving daily,
for the person I wanted to keep by me dearly.

Held hands for the first time, it was magical,
but I could never show how much it meant.....
I wish I could tell u-that moment was mystical !
but my anxiety kept me silent.

The improvement was there but slow,
it was hard but worth to see their face glow.
The past still lurked in the shadows,
but I managed to put them below.

They had waited for this soo long ,
and loved me while I was cold all along,
I was glad to finally show what was in my heart,
rather than putting it aside hurting me more.

ENCHANTED

The next phase was enchanted,
for them-learnt to solve the problems that haunted,
I made sure to subtly say,
"you were the only thing i ever wanted"

I could fight my demons all my life,
if it meant keeping them close by my side.
To explain it was like a trip to the mountains,
where more beautiful than the view-was the ride.

People loved us and why wouldn't they,
made for the fairytale ending that makes people sway.
"In each others arms you both will stay"
that is what the people say..

Enemies to lovers is such a good trope!
and I agree that there was a lot of hope..
this could be our *"happily forever"*
it felt good to be called each others home.

They were the best thing I could ever hope for,
when I resisted love they understood rather than ignore,
they treated me well in all the right ways,
from making me smile to holding the door.

Was never the type to remember birthdays....
but there was a date which in her mind always stays.
tried to wish them at midnight,
but thought it was weird hence didn't despite.

After preparing herself and facing her fear,
finally said *"happy birthday my dear"*
and their smile made them feel sure,
they would never regret overcoming their fear!

Her birthday was never special for her,
she slept through it like a bear.
but the next morning she woke up to see,
a message appeared that she couldn't believe-

A person had stayed up till midnight to wish!
she didn't know she ever deserved all this bliss,
she was used to those cold celebrations...
a wish only with a candy in return.

SMALL THINGS

From being cared under a clause,
to being loved for their flaws.
Someone who noticed me trying,
and never failed to give an applause.

I know loving me is a task pretty hard,
but they did it so well.
Took down all of my guard,
and I opened my wounds,
as I knew I was scarred.

With the dirtiest mind and the sweetest smile,
they were one the most paradoxical beings I had seen in
a while !
I am not the best at recognizing things,
but I bet I can see them coming from a mile.

Like the ocean breeze,
or those late night dreams,
the ones that leave only peace,

and just makes your mind feel at ease.

you are perfect! they used to say,
different from what I was told back in the day,
I couldn't believe how destiny plays!
and how I got what I exactly prayed.

Held my books when my hands felt weak,
and listened for hours as i speak,
the day I slept with a headache ,
made sure there wasn't even a creak!

Whenever felt bad always stayed near,
asking in the softest tone *"you fine dear?"*
I wish I could tell you that meant a lot !!
and that was exactly what I wanted to hear.

Wrote in my pages when I couldn't write,
scolded me for staying up late at night.
always let me go first in the line,
made me feel worthy, almost divine.

THE GOOD OLD TIMES

Shared all my problems while they listened carefully,
as if understanding me was their biggest responsibility.
Listened to my stories all day long,
without ever interrupting or saying wrong.

I had anxiety, pretty bad one,
they gave me playlist filled with songs,
I listen to them till this day when I feel anxious,
I don't know if its the feeling or song which made me
feel safe.

They were the kind to plan the future,
whereas I didn't have a clue,
but for them I started to vision,
my future out of the blue.

The wrapper of the chocolate they gave still has a spot in
my diary,
and so do all the memory,
not even one moment is left,

which I have not carved with my pen.

Still remember the day I finally confessed I loved them,
The first *"I love you,"* soft and shy,
they blushed so hard and never denied...
Eyes cast down, but the smile gave it away,
A moment so bright, it still warms today...

THE CHANGE

I loved them, they loved me...
but night falls after the prettiest beam.
Never thought someone could change so quickly,
but I guess that is what u call destiny....

Still couldn't figure out what went wrong,
spent sleepless night trying to find answers.
Diaries filled with tears and unreleased songs,
heavy heart with feeling I cant transfer.

The words grew colder day by day,
till I was left with nothing to say,
wanted to ask what went wrong,
but didn't want to beg anyone to stay.

Maybe I was hard to love,
Maybe I was just not enough,
Maybe I just made their life tough,
all these thoughts made me never go to them.

The one who would miss everything just to sit with me
and talk,
now made excuses to quietly walk.
the one who wanted to know every detail,
now, didn't even look at my trail.

And you don't know how confusing it gets,
when all of sudden everything resets,
when the past and the present seem too alike,
....and nothing makes sense.

They just did what my old friends did!
left me with not even an inch of guilt.
I tried to be strong and forced a smile,
once again watching pieces of what I had built.

And still I do say don't blame them,
for they made be believe in love again!
but also made me question...
if I was ever worth to be loved then??

WHY?

They were not perfect, neither was I,
just I said all the pain while they chose to hide.
I don't blame them ,but cant justify,
why I fought my demons while they just denied.

When I got close they pulled away,
making me doubt if everything I had been through was
in vain...
don't get them wrong ,they had their battles to play,
but even I did....why couldn't they?

Their withdrawal hurt more than anything else,
when losing them felt like loosing myself,
the worst part was not even that,
it was the dreams decorated in the shelf.

Which were now collecting dust,
as if all just crashed down with a thrust.
things-we can readjust,
but what about the broken trust?

I still can't understand

and maybe I never will

How the person who told me "my biggest regret would be to make you cry"

made me cry the most that I had in my life.

AFTERMATH

After they left I did try my best,
to give my bravest smile with the ache in my chest.
I just did all I could from my side,
and gave them all of the rest.

Once my friends calls me late at night,
in a tone as if she was ready to fight.
"why did she cry? I don't even know"
was what they said I got to know...

maybe they didn't mean it....I don't know,
but some words do leave a blow......

And it just broke my heart into a million pieces,
like the 10yr old who first heard this.
I thought they were different...and maybe they were!
and it was my fate which always brings me back crying
there.

I would've done anything to make them stay,

but after this....I didn't know what to say.
I just sat there wondering *"what even happened?"*
and my past came back just like an array.

I chose to withdraw-became silent,
and not show how my mind had thoughts so violent,
when I saw people around me worried,
plastered a smile without any warrant.

Nobody knew what I really went through,
those months of crying alone in my room,
wondering "to deserve this what harm did I ever do?"
or if my fate was really written in gloom..

All I wanted were the answers to that,
but I couldn't-as I was too scared to ask,
but thanks to my past and thanks to those friends,
I was experienced in tears to mask.

ALL I WANTED

I tried to forget - to let it all fade,
Yet their words still cut like a sharpened blade.
More than the echoes of my past,
hurt the words that they said at last.

I don't regret loving them and I know I never will,
as maybe some part of them needed the love the give.
maybe my part in their life was over,
and useless things are not meant to be kept be it a thing
or a lover.

But there is a bit of anger left in me ,
rather disappointment in how it could be,
if they stayed and didn't run away,
maybe we could have built a future for everyone to see.

All I wanted was for them to not to leave,
no extra time no expensive deals.
All I ever asked for just to love me....
it wasn't that hard.......was it?

I would've waited if you asked for time,
I would've given you everything dime by dime!
but you chose to leave without any sign,
and its fine Right? it is not a crime...

I wonder if they ever even missed me,
Or if I was just a chapter they left so easily,
why i was never good enough to be cherished,
and instead always the one left behind?

HIDDEN

Yet after all this - I waited,
I waited for that one apology, that one talk that never happened,
for them to come back and cherish what we created.

People proposed......I rejected,
waiting for them to come back after they fixed themself.
Didn't want to explain as I was unsure myself,
so I told everyone *"its complicated"*.

And surely it was,
I knew they had some troubles that they used to always hide,
they never told - *but I could read their eyes,*
but whenever I asked they always denied,
didn't want to pressurize so *"ohh ok"* I replied.

I wish they told me all of their pains,
I would've listened with no complaints.

Even if I got covered in blood
I would make sure they didn't have a stain

I still do defend him when world goes cold,
just from a distance ,letting it all unfold.
Don't wanna disturb them so stayed quiet,
even though it echoed - everything they told.

THE REVELATION

After an year of blaming myself,
found out they loved someone else.
"if someone else touched them I will kill Them!" I'd say,
but there I stood-silent and shaken.

I didn't know how to respond,
that feeling was something beyond-
anything I felt to this day,
like a stone thrown into a still pond.

A pond which was an ocean-with terrible waves,
that I had managed to handle and save,
once again back all those faceless memories,
the 10yr old sitting alone in the gallery.

This was my sign to give up on it,
not to date someone else but to hide all the feelings.
to never admit that I wanted them,
and to just accept all the revealings .

First time someone told me "*they're dating someone*",
I told them with confidence "*you must be mistaken!*".
But as people came and repeated the story,
I was left there- shaken.

I thought they would come back .....
come back to me,
*we had been thru so much....**hadn't we?***
for you to just leave as if it was just a fling.

maybe it was......then why give me hopes?
why heal me to just make me worse?
why make promises u cant fulfill?
why fill my life to leave with echoes that chill?

THE REALISATION

That was a phase ever so bad,
to try to forget everything we had.
they broke up....I got the news-a few months back,
"it was nothing serious" they'd add.

I didn't know how to respond to this,
it just didn't seem like they would do something like this.
Maybe they were just searching for something to quiet the ache–
A warmth while everything pulled away.

I hear they look back now with heavy sighs,
Regret tangled in words they'll never say.
It was a thing I cant justify
but humans make mistakes.....don't they?

My friend asked them once,
"*did you know she loved you that much?*"
and to my shock they said no,
they thought to me it didn't matter that much.

And looking back I do realize,
it was because of how I coped.
never once did I openly say ***"don't go"***
he asked can I go and I said yes-

Hoping one day they would find someone better,
still I wanted to tell them to *come back soon.*
But I just stayed quiet looking at the moon,
I wanted to but never told them "I love you" or that "I waited for you"

and that is where the what ifs start......

WHAT IF....

What if I had loved u from the start,
What If I had done my part,
What if I had opened my heart,
What if I had let down my guard.

What if I had told you what I've been thru,
what I care for and the shadows I outgrew.
What if instead of hiding,
I showed u all the scars that still bleed through.

What if when you told you'd leave-I had told u not to.
What if I told u all those words I forgot to.
What if when you said that you were broken,
I chimed in and said me too....

What if I tried express a bit more,
or perhaps to forget what others might think.
What if I told you that you mattered so much,
or without you telling me-understood when u were sore.

What if I confessed that I loved you,
I was waiting for you... *and that maybe I still am !*
What if like you, I shared what I thought,
that I want to spend my life with you....

and....

What if you had not left so easily,
What if you stayed and fought for me,
What if you kept aside your insecurities,
and told me what you felt for me.

What if you had come-when I needed u the most,
What if instead of pulling away-you held me even close.
What if just like you made me feel in the beginning,
you made me feel like someone you were scared to lose.

What If you just came up to me and told what was wrong,
not leave-but fix when you had the time.
What if u understood I waited for you this long !
and come back to me with that special song.

What if you never had that new person.
What if you came and gave me the reason,
of why you did that and what was going on.
What if you didn't make me feel like-

I was just a cure for you boredom.

I know you weren't bad ,neither am I,
but it can't work unless we both try!
and I am done with all those feelings I hide,
so here I am and this is the last of my tries....

I LOVE YOU.....

I love you, I've loved you all along,
but due to my past and fear I couldn't show it at all.
and I know I wasn't the best at the start,
but I can assure you-
pure-were both my intentions and heart.

I know you weren’t trying to hurt me,
Maybe you were just trying to protect yourself ,the only
way you knew how.
but in the process of trying to not hurt,
you *unintentionally* did just that...

Maybe you didn’t mean to pull away.....
you just didn’t know how to stay,
and I know how hard it is to battle yourself everyday !!
one day, you'll win it is the only thing I pray.

If you don't love me just come and make the choice,
that will be last day you hear my voice.
Not as I hate ,trust me I never will,

but just as it is not a choice.....

I won't beg for love, I've done that before,
Yet a part of me waits behind a closed door.
If staying is heavy, I won't make you stay—
If loving me hurts, I'll move out of your way,
as I'd rather lose you than watch us decay.

But if there's a chance, even quiet and small,
I'll be the echo each time that you call.
No malice in me, no blame to be found,
only if you want it, we'll both come around.

And its fine if you never love me,
for my love is not limited to reciprocity.
I've regretted not saying these before all my life,
BUT I LOVE YOU! ....AND NO MORE I WILL HIDE..

FOR YOU....

All I want for you to do is the follows,
if you love me ,tell me to meet where we are the closest,
tell me your part open and honest,
and trust me I'll listen without any malice.

I assure you we will get through this together,
and this flower-Trust me I wont let it wither.
I know you are hurt! no matter how much you hide,
but I promise I'll stay forever.....

But if you don't, it is your choice,
just make sure to say it out and loud.
I would prefer a clear no,
rather than making it die slow.

As of me , if you wonder-
I do love you.
No anger to hold, no ties to sever,
Just hoping we could be together.

I know you think "I deserve better"
but trust me I deserve exactly you!
No perfect words, no love much sweeter,
Just all that you are, and all you do.

I'll cherish what was, no matter how far—
For to me, you'll always be who you are.
But if this is goodbye, I'll let you be free,
No bitterness left—just love quietly.

So tell me now, no fear, no delay—
Do you want me to go or to stay?
I'll honor your truth, whatever you decide,
But know, *my love was never a lie.*

I know I've hurt you in the past unintentionally,
and even you have, that is the irony.
We both know we both never meant to hurt,
and this is the chance to fix what was.

I've loved you, quietly, more than you'll ever know!
I wasn't perfect, I was scared, I made mistakes,
But every feeling for you was real – never fake.

So if there's a part of you that wants me near,
Even if it's small, unsure, unclear –
Say it now, with no disguise,

I’ll meet you there — no questions, no lies.

Whatever you choose, I’ll understand,
No pressure, no push, just an open hand.
But know this love is honest and deep,
A promise to give, not a vow to keep.

I won’t ever hold on if you want to be free,
But if you want a chance just call me.
No matter the answer, I’ll always care,
But I won’t wait for a love if it isn't there

I won’t chase what isn’t mine to hold,
But my heart stays warm, never cold.
If you want me to stay, just say it true—
I’ll stay forever!, but only if it’s me you choose.

And if you’re unsure right now,
just tell me to wait.
I’ll understand, I swear.
please don’t leave me hanging,
don’t stay silent —

if you don't love me,
just say it loud to my face "I'll never love you!"
and if you do-
I promise I'll make sure this turns into something beautiful .

That's all I ask.

I hope you make a choice you don't regret
its your life and u have the choice
and I will let you pick!